T0131686

THE SIMPLE SOLUTION

MARK WHITE

authorHOUSE®

AuthorHouse™
1663 Liberty Drive
Bloomington, IN 47403
www.authorhouse.com
Phone: 1 (800) 839-8640

Published by AuthorHouse   03/17/2020

ISBN: 978-1-7283-5100-1 (sc)
ISBN: 978-1-7283-5099-8 (e)

Print information available on the last page.

PREFACE

What is the answer? A question that many people have either tried to answer, or find the answer to. What is life? Why am I here? What will give me fulfillment, and purpose. Why isn't everyday of my life the best day of my life? What's ahead in my future? What happens after life? If God exist, then why does He watch all of the terrible things happen and do nothing? I could go on and on with the many questions that billions upon billions of people have wanted the answers to. This book was written to address some questions that many people have asked. Also to expose a hidden truth that is so simple, it gets overlooked billions a time a day. The most complex problems that we can ever face, all surprisingly have the most simplest solution. Once there is a solution to a problem, then it cease from being a problem. Funny thing is, is that there has never been a problem that didn't have a simple solution. The thing is that to some they have made the problem bigger than the solution. The most successful people to have ever lived all had this in common, they never perceived a problem, to big for a SOLUTION.

CHAPTER ONE

DON'T GIVE UP

The very first step to finding the solution is, to never stop believing that there is a solution. We live in an age where humanity has discovered medicines, technology, information that has provided solutions to challenges that mankind has faced for thousands of years. Why do we have such things as telephones, computers, cures for diseases etc. Was it because there were no challenges? Did these things just come together by chance? Did someone have a magic wand and (poof) these things occurred? Or did all of a sudden the events just so happen to co-exist and create any of these things? No, no and as many times as you can try to imagine that NO! Nothing just happens. These things happened because somewhere, someone was determined to do whatever it took despite any doubt, challenge, obstacle; its simply because they wouldn't give up. YES its that simple. If no matter what life throws your way you determine that you wont quit. That your life and existence both have a meaning more than just pain and problems with no solution. That if I didn't get it today, then rest and tomorrow will answer for yesterday. Yesterday will explain my future. How is that? Well if you really look back at all your yesterdays, you can understand why the present is wherever it is. In other words whatever you do today will determine where your future is headed. I promise you this one thing that the only thing that will ever be able to hold you back is you. Situations, people, circumstances, obstacles nothing has the power to stop you. It is only at the point you quit, you lose. You see we were all born with the same thing. Different races, ideas, cultures but we all have this in common..........

A CHOICE. Giving up is a choice. When you have been pushed, pulled, leaned on, betrayed, misused, abused or anything life throws your way. The one thing life, people, or any situation that comes cannot do is choose for you. You have to make the choice to fight or quit. The first step to finding the solution to life's toughest problems is to buckle down, stand firm, despite all and DON'T QUIT! (suicide is not an option).

CHAPTER TWO

✻ ⎯⎯⊰⊹ ⊹⊱⎯⎯ ✻

LET THERE BE LIGHT

The very first words to ever be spoken was LET THERE BE LIGHT. WHY? Why not the sun or the moon? Why not truth, love, compassion? Why not peace, nor harmony? One definition for lights is: The natural agent that stimulates sight and makes things visible. Another definition states: Understanding of a problem or mystery, enlightenment. The bible says that in the beginning God created the heavens and the earth. Even though everything was dark and void God still created. Then why did he say let there be light. God didn't need the light to create so why did he say these words. John 1:1-4 will explain. God said these words so that mankind would have that visible, understanding to every mystery, or challenge. To see the solution for the darkness. Lets read that: In the beginning was the Word, and the Word was with God, and the Word was God. The same was in the beginning with God. All things were made by Him and without Him was not anything made that was made. In Him was life; and the life was the light of men. Genesis 1:3 (and God said let there be light). The light of men came at the Word of God. The reason why some cant find the answers they seek is because they wont accept the light. The only way to see the light, is to realize the light came forth through Gods Word. Psalms 119:105 says Thy Word is a lamp unto my feet and a light unto my path. Plain and simple the Words that come from the Mouth of God is what gives mankind light. Well some might say the bible was written by men. Played with, changed words, etc. In just my few years of existence I have never experienced a lie, secret, sin, even wrongful thoughts or wishes that were not exposed. Because time after countless time whatever is done in the dark comes back to those first spoken words(LET THERE BE LIGHT)!!!!! No one has ever came forth and proven in all these years, that the bible has been written, and exposed it as a lie. Just in our generation presidents, business, even pastors and men of God have all been exposed for being something less than the truth. You can go back in history and one thing is certain. Good or bad has been exposed because before

God created a sun or moon, He made the light shine in a very dark place to light the way for all men to see. Lets try a brief but powerful exercise or better yet lets call it an example. Take a look around at your surroundings very good. Pick 3 items in you mind. Make sure they are in three different locations. Study where they are. Okay now close your eyes and try to go find each item(no peeking). When you finish open your eyes, and flip the page for a shocking, but simple solution:(TRUTH).

THAT'S YOUR LIFE WITHOUT THE LIGHT

CHAPTER THREE

❊ ━━━ ◅┼ ┼▻ ━━━ ❊

THE MEANING OF LIFE

Why are there such things as human beings on this place called earth? Well if you have made it this far, then I'm sure you're interested in truth. Genesis 1:26 And God said, Let us make man in our image, after our likeness, and let them have dominion: I want to pause in this passage of scripture right here. If you were to go back to the beginning you will find that God created heaven and earth. He then, with His Mouth began to bring into existence everything we see and don't see. So that everything God spoke happened. Then on the sixth day, after preparing every necessity for the survival and existence of the earth. Vegetation, animal kind, and man kind. He then takes His Spirit, His Word, and reaches down with his hand and forms a man. For He said let Us. Every person is made in the image of God. We have a spirit which will live forever. The only way that man came to life was when God breathe into his nostrils (Genesis 2:7). Before that he was just an empty shell. Not even oxygen could bring him to life, and yes there was oxygen because the animals had to breathe. We exist today only because God breathe into us a part of Him. That yearning deep inside often times gets ignored. That is why you can achieve many great feats in life and still feel empty. Simply because many people ignore the very essence of our existence. I want to define essence: the intrinsic nature or indispensable quality of something, especially something abstract, that determines its character. You cannot put a ford motor in a Chevrolet, Its not designed to work that way. The meaning of life is in your purpose in life. You were to function a certain way. Only the designer of anything understands how it was made to work. Every solution in life will be found in only one place.

THE SOURCE

CHAPTER FOUR

FULLFILMENT

Everything in life reaches its fullest potential, when it follows the guidelines of how it was created to operate. A fish cannot operate effectively on land, because it wasn't created for that. Everyone has a different purpose in life. Its when you are operating the way that you, not imitating anyone else, but how you were designed to function. That is the moment you reach fulfillment. This does not mean that problems wont exist. You were created in the Image of God so a problem always has a solution. There was a reason God told Adam not to eat from that tree (Genesis 2:16-17). There was no limitation on anything in the garden.(WHY). Then God proceeds to tell him that the day you do this you will die(WHY). Well first of all, it was the tree of the knowledge of good and evil. Before then mans only knowledge came from God. God walked and talked with man every day. Man gained the knowledge of evil that day. Best believe he didn't get it from God. There were no such things as death, disease, murder. Man was complete, fulfilled. It wasn't until man wanted his own knowledge, that God withdrew his presence. God cannot tolerate sin in his presence, He is Holy. Without Gods Presence man lost the very Breath of God which brought his inner being to life. The bible says in Genesis 3:8 that after man ate from the tree. When God came looking for them, that they hid from the presence of God. There eyes were open and the one thing that made them stand boldly before God was now gone. In other words he lost his fulfillment. A fish cannot be complete without the presence of water. He is no longer fulfilled, he begins to die. The definition of fulfilled simply is: to bring to completion or reality, achieve or realize(something desired, promised, or predicated). It simply means to be wanting nothing. It is every persons desire to win. No one actually sets out to fail at anything that they give effort to. We are made in Gods Image. The problem is our nature does not know how. We have a sin nature and nothing about sin knows how to win. This is why we need our nature to conform to our Image. How does one accomplish that? Its simple. Before sin Adam spent his time gaining knowledge from the Creator of all things. Let me put it like this, if you were interested in becoming rich. Where would you seek knowledge? You see Adam was in the one place that no one will ever fail. Why do I say you cant fail? Bill Gates could tell you about being rich, but there are some areas of life even he couldn't answer. Adam didn't even fear when God brought all the massive animals to him to name. He was connected to the most important relationship ever to man. I tell you what, you put your (blank) desire in the blank and I can make you this promise. If what you desire is not evil God has the answer. Yes its that simple. He made everything even the modern day medicine and technology that we human beings have just really learned. Adam was in the only sure place that any human will ever find true fulfillment: in the presence of God. When one finds their purpose, there is no greater fulfillment. God knows you, your purpose and destiny. We even talk to therapist spend money to try and get answers to questions, that all God wants is what he and Adam had. One on one talks with His children, answering our questions. Fulfillment is simply a life with no limitations, because every area of your life is full wanting nothing. You cannot want in God's Presence.

CHAPTER FIVE

NAKED AND ASHAMED

WHY ARE THERE TOUGH TIMES?

Genesis 3:10 And he said I heard thy voice in the garden, and I was afraid, because I was naked, and I hid myself. Ashamed: embarrassed or guilty because of ones actions, characteristics, or associations. Another definition says: reluctant to do something through fear of embarrassment or humiliation. If you go back to Genesis 2:25 it says: And they were both naked the man and his wife, and were not ashamed. What's my point? ITS SIMPLE! Man was clothed with the Glory of God. There were no fears, insecurities, doubts. Gods Spirit shined so bright in man, that there were no weakness and, imperfection. When everything in Gods creation looked at man, they saw the Light of God and submitted to the glory that was placed to cover man from his nakedness. Adam never had to worry about a lion, or any creature you can think of seeing him as food. God brought the animals to Adam to name (Genesis 2:19). Adam was in the position that God first intended for man. Something happened that changed all that. To explain this I must share a little history. A mutiny broke out in heaven. God created an angel named lucifer and made him a thing of beauty. Mind you now angels were created to fulfill Gods purpose without a choice. Lucifer was covered with many stones to reflect Gods Glory. He was the leader of praise and worship unto God. He began to feel pride. He starts discord in heaven and convinces a third of heaven that God was unfair. That they had a right to choose and not be governed by His law. Lucifer is then thrown out and now looking for a place that he can rule as God rules. Then God decides to create a weaker, physical version of Himself. Even in some ways weaker than the very angels. God then decides to give us something that is so misunderstood that the simplest part of it is overlooked. He gave us free will (WHY). Because there is nothing better in time or eternity, this world or the next. It is when someone loves you because they choose to!!!! Not out of force or because need of benefit. There is nothing more powerful to exist than love. When Adam broke Gods Will he didn't realize that that's all lucifer needed to have his way in the place that God gave man to rule. You see when their eyes were opened they actually saw themselves, not the Glory that God placed on them. Its almost like being very wealthy and secure. You have the respect of everything around you. All of a sudden you loose everything. Bank account empty, home reposed, all because you listened to the advice of someone lesser than you. That was out to get you all the time. The very first thing you would do is get somewhere and hide. So why are there tough times? ITS SIMPLE! Its because Adam gave everything that God intended for us to have in just one decision. He gave lucifer the power that day and whoever has the power makes the rules. This is the very reason why there is so much evil in the world today.

CHAPTER SIX

WHY BOTHER

WHATS THE USE

If satan took the power from us then why bother? St. John 3:16 For God so loved the world that He GAVE His only begotten Son, that whosoever believeth in Him should not perish but have everlasting life. Its evident that God is not selfish, or why would He want to create beings to share in His creation. Not only did He give us our own choice, but He even made provisions to fix the wrong choices He knew we would make. Lucifer's fate is already set, so he is trying everything he can to destroy yours. Have you ever heard the saying misery loves company. One of his main objectives is to convince as many people as possible, to not believe in the last passage of scripture that we read. Satan understands the depth of Gods Love. He also knows the rewards prepared for those who choose to believe in Gods Word. So to get back at God for His unconditional love for us, he is bent on trying to rob every human being of what God has prepared for us through the gift of His Son (His Word). St. John 10:10 The thief cometh not, but for to steal, and to kill, and to destroy: I am come that they (you) might have life, and that they (you) might have it more abundantly. Why should a person bother well its simple. Anyone who is willing to give there very life to save yours. Let me put it to you like this: Imagine that you've committed a unforgivable crime which by law required the death penalty. Your dad loved you so much that on the day of your judgement He His very own self came into the court room and took your place. He really and I mean really literally died so that you might live. Why should a person bother, who wouldn't for a dad that loves and protect his child like that. A majority of the world is bent on keeping people from believing in Jesus Christ. Satan will try everything to stop you from receiving Jesus Christ (GODS WORD) as your personal Lord and Savior (WHY). That's simple too. He's going down and he wants everyone that will be foolish enough to follow him. Proverbs 14:1 The fool hath said in his heart, There is no God. IF there isn't anything else in this world that you would ever consider please and I really mean please consider what I am saying to you right now. If you don't accept the same Word, the Light that god sent to die in your place. Then satan has robbed you of what God invested to save you. If your child died for someone else who act like he did nothing at all for them (Wow). God only intended for lucifer and his rebellion to live in hell for eternity. Honestly how would you feel if your child was wrongfully sentenced for what someone else did who really didn't care. Why live here on earth and face all the hell that life puts you through to die and go to an everlasting hell.

CHAPTER SEVEN

FREEDOM

SALVATION

Romans 10:8-10 But what saith it? The Word is nigh thee, even in thy mouth, and in thy heart: that is, the word of faith, which we preach. That if thou shalt confess with thy mouth the Lord Jesus, and shall believe in thine heart that God hath raised Him from the dead, thou shalt be saved. For with the heart man believeth unto righteousness: and with the mouth confession made unto salvation. What does it mean to be free. One definition says: not restrained, obstructed, or fixed; unimpeded. Another says: released from captivity, confinement or slavery. I really like this one best: to cause or allow someone or something to stop having or being affected by something unpleasant, painful, or unwanted. God sent His Son so that we could be free of the unpleasant, painful and unwanted circumstances of sin. God set it up so that by the same way he brought everything into existence, the same way we can be free from what sin has done to this world. With the words of our mouth, and what we believe in our hearts. Yes its that simple. If what you have read so far has made sense to you, then pray this prayer out loud. Lord Jesus I confess with my mouth that you gave your very life for my salvation. I believe in my heart that God raised You from the dead. I ask that you would come into my heart, my trust, my very life to You right now in Jesus Name amen. If you have prayed that prayer and believe you now have an everlasting glorious future.

CHAPTER EIGHT

❖ ━━◆─ ─◆━━ ❖

THE MOUTH

NO EXPLAINATION NEEDED

If all I had to do was say it, then why are so many Christians living stressed, confused, angry, basically a defeated life? Its simple. Proverbs 18:21 Death and Life are in the power of the tongue: and they that love it shall eat the fruit thereof. If you have made it this far then you already know that we were made in the Image of God. Exactly how did god create everything except for us. With His Word. I use to say all the time that when the seasons change that I would be sick, and sure enough every season change guess what. Your mouth will create whatever comes out of it, just like when God said let there be light there was light. I guarantee you that no successful person that worked for his success walked around using words like: I'll never make it. I'm not good enough. I don't have what it takes. (Why)? Its simple they talked the way they believed. God gave us a very powerful, creative gift. The sad part is that there are some Christians who read there bibles and take this scripture so lightly. I'm not saying that there wont be problems, but if you keep believing and speaking, especially what the Word of God says nothing and I mean nothing can stop you from having what you say. Just know that lucifer is going to try everything to get you to stop believing, stop saying, but know this also; that no one can stop a person that wont quit. Your words are so important because we were made in Gods Image. John 1:1-3 says; In the beginning was the Word and the Word was with God, and the Word was God. The same was in the beginning. All things were made by Him, and without Him was not anything made. God set up a system by which all things were created. Then He created us to be like Him. Satan hates you because of this. When God brought all the creatures to Adam, whatever came out of Adams mouth that's what that creature was. God could have told Adam what He wanted everything to be called, but He made us to have dominion here. Why are your words so important? Its simple; because God set laws and principles in His creation of things. Gravity is a law. Night and day is a law He set into motion. Every tree bears seed within itself to keep producing. God wanted Adam to do as he did. Speak what things were to be. Same principle used to create everything. if you really want to live that abundant life that Jesus came for us to have then you will have to be careful of your words. You have creative power in your mouth

CHAPTER NINE

MIND GAMES

SATAN'S TACTICS

Philippians 4:8 Finally my brethren, whatsoever things are true, whatsoever thins are honest, whatsoever things are just, whatsoever things are pure, whatsoever things are lovely, whatsoever things are of a good report, if there be any virtue, and if there be any praise, THINK on these things. (Think): direct ones mind toward someone or something; use ones mind actively to form connected ideas. Because God gave us all free will we are responsible for making our own choices. God and satan are trying to do the very same thing. God set free will into motion so He cannot force you. just as well satan cant either.

Their both trying to influence you. God wants the very best for you so He works throughout your lifetime to persuade you to make the right choices. I think by now we know what satan is trying to do. It all starts with your thoughts. This is why the writer of this scripture gives you a very simple way to have more victory in life. The mind is a very important part of our existence. One of satans greatest tricks is to get you to doubt yourself. Luke 4:3 And the devil said unto Him (Jesus) If thou be the son of God. If he can get you to reason with yourself, or change your thought process, then you are on your way to making the same mistake Adam made. Any successful person and I guarantee that when they faced adversity or uncertainty, the thing that kept them afloat was that they kept thinking positively. Before you can formulate words that bring negativity it starts in your mind. How does a person overcome the mind games that the enemy uses to defeat us? ITS SIMPLE: (Philippians 4:8) but if you never read and study your bible, then when you are under attack you wont know how to combat against the enemy. Go back to Luke 4 and you will find with every temptation Jesus replied (It is written). If you don't feed your brain the Word of God then how will you ever be able to defeat the craftiness of the devil. If you spend your time watching T.V., playing video games, on your mobile devices then you have fallen for one of the enemies greatest tactic today. Adam and Eve got there attention turned to the tree instead of Gods Word and look what happened. If T.V. or anything else gets more of you attention. Your job, kids if anything comes before the time you spend with God, then you have the answer to why the devil seems to get the best of you. A person that studies in a certain field normally becomes great at it with hard work and study. A person that spends his time in the Word of God, who also spends time with God asking for wisdom and understanding. That person will become an overcomer. If you ask Bill Gates how to run a multi-billion dollar company, he could tell you because he has studied countless time after time until it became second nature. He probably doesn't even have to think to answer any question you could have. If you were to ask God how to win in this life then He would lead you to the BASIC   INSTRUCTIONS   BEFORE LEAVING   EARTH Plain and simple the (BIBLE). Feed your mind something that can actually help you not foolishness and your life will change dramatically.

CHAPTER TEN

PRAYER

YOUR PERSONAL PHONE LINE TO GOD

St. Luke 18:1 And He spake a parable unto them to this end, that men ought always to pray, and not to faint. One of the most things in any relationship is communication. Marriages with no communication often fail. In a home where children and parents don't communicate, there's often problems. Children often get into lots of trouble or make plenty of mistakes in life when they devalue communication, and advise from their older and wiser parents. Its sad to say, but I too could have avoided a lot of misery, and heartache if I had only applied the advice from my parents, and everyone who loved me enough to tell me the truth. Do you know why there's a high ratio of wealthy people's children who have success with money? Its simple, its because at some point they spent time listening and learning from their older and wiser parents. Its crazy how so many people look for life's answers, and overlook the fact that the best one to answer these questions is the giver of life. If you really wanted to know the inspiration for your favorite song, who better to ask than the writer of that song. If you want to know the answer to questions that seem to have no answer for you UM............DUH! Yes its just that simple. Here's the thing: the closest relationships that you ever see are the ones that communicate the most. How would you feel if you were in a relationship, marriage, parental, or either just a plain old friendship, that only come around when they need something. That would not get the best from you, especially when you've given more. Well here's another DUH moment; there will never be any other greater love that any human being will ever possess, than the Love of God. God knows the answer to all of life's problems. The craziest thing is that He actually wants to answer those questions, but sad to say a lot of people don't talk to, or hardly talk Him. God loves you so much but He's not going to force Himself on you. Why pray: (IT'S SMPLE) because no one will ever want better for you, no one will ever know you better than God. No one will ever be able to look beyond our faults, yes I said ours because we all have faults, and love us enough to give us to give us His ever unfailing Word to die for us. Yes the very Word that spoke everything that exist died despite knowing the mistakes we would make. Isaiah 46:9-10 Remember the former things of old, for I am God, and there is none else; I am God, and there is none like Me. Declaring the end from the beginning, and from ancient times the things that are not yet done, saying My Counsel shall stand, and I will do My Pleasure. It would be very foolish not to talk to Someone who would go to those lengths for you. to know your every move before you make one, and still choose to love and die for you. One that knows every single detail about you, also knows what will work for you. That relationship my friends, would simplify all of our lives.

CHAPTER ELEVEN

LOVE

LIFES ANSWER

1 John 4:8 He that loveth not knoweth not God; for God is love. How can I say that this is the answer to life? Well once again ITS SIMPLE. God is love. If there was more love in the world today there would be less problems. Once again God is love. If there was more God in this world there would be less problems. Problems came because of sin. Sin came because of jealousy and pride. There is no pride in love. Love is unselfish. In your spare time read 1 Corinthians 13. True love doesn't care about advantage or disadvantage. True love only wants what is best. You see when you love someone, even if they are

wrong you still want what's best for them. People with children really understand this. This is how much Jesus loved us. One of the biggest problems with the world today, is that self has to get credit. This is what satan did. Anytime you or your feelings are more important than anything else, then you are in pride. It took love for God to create us, knowing already what we would do. It took love for Jesus to give His life, that He died even for those who will reject His offering. I believe that the day we stand before God, that a lot of people will try to bring up all of the good that they think they have done. I also believe that God's reply will be (WHY?). If your answer, or better yet your motive was not because of love, God will not be pleased. One definition of love says: The true Nature of God. I also believe when He ask about the wrongs most answers will be similar to Adam's and Eve's. They did this so I did that. God will not judge you on the basis of what someone else did. Do you realize how difficult it was for Jesus to be spit upon, punched in the face, publicly humiliated. How about being whipped until the flesh was ripped from His body. To take the blame for something He didn't do. To have nails, and I don't mean household nails, driven thru His hands and feet. To have a crown of thorns shoved onto His head. To have the power to prevent it but allow it for the sake of someone else. In this world we live in now, we cant even stand a little criticism much less suffer for the sake of another. You might say but what about the intentions of others, crime, poverty, wars how am I supposed to love? Romans 13:8-10. Owe no man anything, but to love one another: for he that loveth another hath fulfilled the law. For this, Thou shall not commit adultery, Thou shall not kill, Thou shall not steal, Thou shall not bear false witness, thou shall not covet, and if there be any other commandment, it is briefly comprehended in this saying, namely, Thou shall love thy neighbor as thyself. Love worketh no ill to his neighbor: therefore love is the fulfilling of the law. Where there is love all of these things couldn't exist. There will be no poverty, sickness, diseases in Heaven. No envy, hatred, jealousy. Why are children killed, raped, abused, because a lack of love. Why is there poverty, because most that could change things love themselves more. Love saw the condition of the world before it began. Saw that we were helpless. Decided to leave the glory, riches, peace, honor, and harmony in Heaven, to come down and do something for those who couldn't. Do you want to know what will change the world? ITS SIMPLE! Just by loving you can begin a change that will reap eternal rewards. You might say how can I love. It's very I mean very simple. Thou shall love thy neighbor as thyself. No way you would hurt yourself even if you were wrong. No way you would take, abuse, or any other hurtful thing to yourself even if

CHAPTER TWELVE

THE SIMPLE SOLUTION

IT'S REALLY NOT THAT COMPLICATED

Well this will be the last and final chapter. My prayer is that some way, wherever you are in the world that this book will begin a change in your life. Life can be very complicated, but the solutions are simple to every problem, trial, test, pain and any other situation that challenges you. Once you realize that its not as difficult as it seems, then you are ready to live a stress free liberated life. Matthew 11:28-30 (The words of Jesus) Come unto me, all ye that labor and are heavy laden, and I will give you rest. Take My yoke upon you, and learn of Me, for I am meek and lowly in heart; and ye shall find rest unto your souls. For my yoke is easy, and my burden is light. Laden: heavily loaded or weighed down. Another definition says: loaded heavily with something; having or carrying a large amount of something. If at all possible satan will try his best to burden you, pressure you, and push you beyond your measure. There is great news though. Jesus died to give us back liberty. To free us from every burden, sickness, and every sin that so easily beset us. How can you find simplicity in this very complicated world? I think by now you know the next statement: ITS SIMPLE. Jesus said for every worry, worn out, beat down, pressed down, feeling like giving up situation you face, all you have to do is come unto Him. 1 Peter 5:7 Cast all your care upon Him; for He careth for you. Once you can get to the point that you realize that God loves you, He's there for you, and waiting for you to give Him you problems, then your complicated life will begin to simplify. God is the creator. What most people don't know is Before He created the world and every thing in it, He created the solution to every thing He knew would go wrong. Any problems you face does not surprise God. He made a plan for your life before He created anything. Before man sinned there was to be no sickness, but being an all knowing God, He created our bodies to heal themselves. Whenever you get a fever that is your body heating up to fight off infection. If there had never been sin there would not have been so much as a common cold. God being that wise has every answer that you will ever need. Will life get challenging sometimes? YES! Will you experience pain sometimes? YES! John 6:33 (the words of Jesus) These things I have spoken unto you, that in me ye might have peace. In the world ye shall have tribulation: but be of good cheer; I have overcome the world. I want to leave you with a few simple solutions that I have found to help me through life:

(1) No matter what life throws your way don't ever and I mean ever give up.

(2) As a result of not giving up you will see the light shine on your life and all its situations.

(3) The light will begin to explain the meaning and purpose for your life.

(4) Knowing one's purpose will always give you the fulfillment you need.

(5) Being fulfilled reverses the curse of being naked and ashamed.

(6) Once the shame is gone life wont bother as much despite the challenges that will come.

(7) Freedom: the power or right to act, speak, or think as one wants without hinderance or restraint. In Jesus there is true freedom.

(8) Even though there is freedom don't forget your words create your world.

(9)   Keep and guard your mind this is the place where satan comes to attack you.

(10) You must as a necessity pray and talk to God every day.

(11) Make it a purpose to love every day no matter how difficult it gets continue to love.

(12) Once you apply these principles your complicated life will start to become simpler. May the grace and favor of our God cover you in everything you do. In the Mighty name of Jesus amen.

Printed in the United States
By Bookmasters